MW01517308

Eric M. Brodsky

Poetry of the Angels II

Inspiration For Us All

Universal One Publishers
Broomfield, Colorado

FIRST EDITION

Published for
Universal One Publishers
370 Interlocken Blvd. 4th Fl.
Broomfield, CO 80021

A percentage of net proceeds goes to support
The Universal One Foundation.

Cover Layout and Design:
Deborah Hill, Malaya Creations
www.onlinecreative.com

Library of Congress Card Number:
00-191433

ISBN 0-9676406-3-6

First printing August, 2000
10 9 8 7 6 5 4 3 2 1

BIOGRAPHY

Eric M. Brodsky is the founder of The Universal One Foundation and president of Universal One Publishers. These "non-profit" and "for-profit" companies serve to provide love and inspiration through free services and retail print materials. Eric offers inspirational lectures, seminars and group workshops to businesses, stores, expos, and private groups, without requiring any fee. Messages of Love come through Eric for free; it is in this same way that he chooses to share them.

By experiencing these Universal messages, thousands of people of all ages have chosen to replace their frustrations and fears, with greater peace and love. The sharing of these simple messages acts as a guide to mental freedom and Self-empowerment.

FOREWORD

It is such a privilege,
and honor to share,
the Love flowing through,
with beings everywhere.
Thanks to each of you,
for this book's creation,
I'm Inspired to be a vehicle,
of such joy and elation.

This book is the second,
of a trilogy,
that requires openness,
for your Truth to see.
Presented they are now,
for children and adults,
may this Wisdom lead,
to Inspiring results.

CONTENTS

INTRODUCTION

This glorious book was written,
as a Spirit collaboration,
Wisdom conveyed as poetry,
to Inspire mass elation.
Some messages are simple,
while others are profound,
listen with an open mind,
for in-sight to resound.

This book is a Loving guide,
to find Self-Love within,
where fears are transmuted,
letting happiness begin.
This book is our Loving gift,
where we hope you find,
an increase in clarity,
and freedom of the mind.

DEDICATION

To the Universal One,
this book "We" dedicate,
comprising All existence,
which few can negate.
Your glorious existence,
as part of the "Whole",
project love into this book,
an equally important role.

You're all so very beautiful,
you've come so very far,
allow this text to guide you,
and remind you Who You Are.
Your life may have confusion,
"We" offer Love and peace,
to bring about your clarity,
from disorder's release.

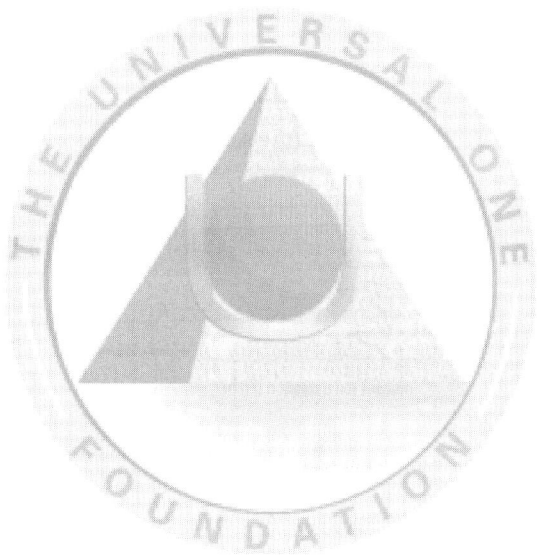

THE
UNIVERSAL ONE

God and void energies,
were the very start,
until the Father/Mother,
"birthed" a single "part".
This spherical "egg" of Light,
as The Love extension,
expanded out like a bang,
into The first "invention".

These energies of God,
"Our" Universal start,
as One Love connection,
family "We" are part.
Free-will manifesting,
creates diversity,
regardless of appearance,
One We'll always be.

UNIVERSAL LOVE

Sending Love to everyone,
in an equal way,
is sharing high vibrations,
without mental sway.
This "Light" illumines darkness,
shows forgotten Love,
it unifies all consciousness,
as One with "above".

This process will be easier,
when you can accept,
your-Self without judgment,
for sharing-skills adept.
Send your Loving thoughts,
there's no required touch,
no force can be perceived,
yet they will do much.

PEACE

Dear BeLoved angels,
a "Master key" is peace,
foundation of True happiness,
catalyst for release.
It disperses any thoughts,
you have within your mind,
it leads to True listening,
where depth you will find.

To be in mental peace,
you may be anywhere,
no mountain tops required,
relaxation is the care.
Focus in that moment,
listen to everything,
immerse within that beauty,
Our "voices" you will bring.

RELAXATION

Peace and relaxation,
are both intertwined,
relaxing is more physical,
while peace is of the mind.
All types of relaxation,
are stillness you begin,
starting with the body,
then mentalness comes in.

It will help to find,
a non-distraction place,
turn off tv's and phones,
less disruptions you will face.
To relax your mind,
focus on the "now",
release past or future "noise",
"vacations" you allow.

LISTENING

To listen is to focus,
on the Voice within,
that guides all experience,
of chosen discipline.
When you begin to listen,
and flow with Love and peace,
you hear your Self-desires,
understanding will increase.

To begin your listening,
start with peace of mind,
reducing mental "busy-ness",
is clarity you'll find.
Listening does not only,
refer to spoken word,
listen "in between the lines"
for silence to be heard.

VALIDATION

To validate experiences,
perceived by the brain,
determine the True clarity,
you consciously sustain.
There will be vast extremes,
with drugs or lack thereof,
as well as with emotions,
versus flowing Love.

Each has a "little voice",
entirely unique,
with their Faithful following,
Self-confidence can peak.
Only you determine,
Truth in what you hear,
some clear trial followings,
remove this doubting fear.

REMINDERS

A reminder is a jolt,
another sends to you,
to expand awareness,
for the current view.
Hearing the reminders,
from within your "head",
can be of Self-connection,
where clarity will shed.

If you do not worry,
of things to memorize,
reminders flow from Spirit,
as memory amplifies.
Reminders are eternal,
to assist your flow,
with your experiences,
for greater ease to Know.

FOCUS

To maximize experience,
and honor Self that's True,
focus in a "Whole" way,
on everything you do.
Splitting up attention,
between many events,
divides creative Power,
understanding it prevents.

By living life with focus,
depth you will see,
more passion in experience,
more joy there will be.
By being "completely" present,
life becomes more clear,
distractions lost enable,
more "progress" to appear.

BUSY-NESS

Keeping your mind busy,
without thinking rest,
works all your body,
where it becomes distressed.
No matter what the cause,
or importance you believe,
without a peaceful balance,
dis-ease you will receive.

The belief money supports,
your business or your kin,
without your health or presence,
is deception you begin.
"Busy-ness" has many goals,
like freedom, joy or peace,
they will attract more quickly,
when you allow release.

UNDERSTANDING

Many levels of understanding,
are perceived by the mind,
from vocabulary meanings,
to the experiential kind.
For greatest understanding,
in this ever-changing place,
let listening and experience,
joyfully interlace.

After you have listened,
obtaining your direction,
your mind will be translator,
for experience erection.
Whether always Known,
or explained by a Soul,
True understanding comes,
from the Experiential role.

WORDS

Words mean very little,
without supportive action,
they guide as "stepping stones",
to mental satisfaction.
They also can remind,
of what you forgot,
follow words with action,
that's what means "a lot".

Experiencing in depth,
can have you "tongue tied",
words are so limiting,
interaction must be tried.
Like the words you read,
that may help or guide,
the only way to understand,
is for them to be applied.

EXPERIENCE

You memorize the words,
or believe you understand,
yet experience is the meaning,
of life each has planned.
No one can ever tell you,
the way that you will feel,
unique is your experience,
and that which is real.

With bodies for experience,
and expressions too,
joyfully embrace them all,
as creations by you.
Each experience is a step,
towards a new plateau,
as goals become closer,
more joys you will Know.

LEVELS

Levels are for experience,
providing foundations,
as courses to prepare you,
for flow of your creations.
From any relationship,
to Awareness you build,
without some progression,
weakness you've instilled.

If you've chosen Love,
as path you desire,
gradually cells transform,
to vibrations that're higher.
Your bodies are adjusting,
to every thought you send,
amassing from the levels,
with focus you intend.

TRUTH

All references to "Truth",
are Wisdom from "above",
connected to the Spirit-Self,
All part of God's Love.
Truth holds no illusion,
it's shared eternally,
the amount received will vary,
by how open you can be.

There are vast extremes,
of Truth each receives,
some are Universal,
others "no one" believes.
None can state your Truth,
it must be Self-achieved,
only you possess this map,
where "Treasures" are retrieved.

SELF-EMPOWERMENT

Being Self-empowered,
is Knowing Who You Are,
living life as you choose,
connected with "Afar".
This consciousness of Spirit,
partners "Us" with you,
you follow Self-desires,
with a focused view.

The more Self-empowered,
the more you can lead,
with this Loving guidance,
this planet you will seed.
Enjoy your Self-connection,
as freely as you Know,
nothing is impossible,
let imagination flow.

HONESTY

For understanding honesty,
within you must go,
the more direct you choose,
more Truth you will Know.
There are clever people,
who can manipulate,
deception with honesty,
illusions they create.

Some conform with "masks",
for ulterior gain,
in friendship or business,
deceit they sustain.
Be True to ThySelf,
to Know Who You Are,
mix this with experience,
goals are not as far.

KNOWING

Knowing is Faith extreme,
where doubt cannot exist,
there's nothing to question,
as fears do not persist.
It can be subconscious,
where some instinctly Know,
yet they do not realize,
they're in the Spirit flow.

You see through illusion,
and "heal" with great ease,
life becomes more joyful,
with Faith to n'th degrees.
To really understand,
you must live in Truth,
this is conscious Power,
where the flow is smooth.

POWER

The Wisdom you acKnowledge,
is Power you obtain,
with this Love connection,
Strength you will gain.
The clarity you possess,
varies the Loving flow,
which determines the intensity,
of Power that you Know.

As the planet changes,
more will try to seek,
tricks of the Awareness,
with a mind that's weak.
Some change from excess ego,
as fear reduces Power,
keep Love as the Only Source,
your Abilities will flower.

WALKING
YOUR TALK

This "new age" Awareness,
has brought many out,
"prophets" knowing words,
while actions are in "doubt".
May you choose to see,
the charlatans of the day,
who feed on monetary needs,
and not the Loving way.

Whatever path you choose,
live what you teach,
combine Love and passion,
the Universe you reach.
You are like a teacher,
everywhere you go,
"walking the talk" anywhere,
is guidance that you show.

MANIFESTING

Every being is a master,
of their universe,
where anything is possible,
with fears in reverse.
Whatever you focus on,
it becomes more real,
the rate which it manifests,
comes from Love and zeal.

You will not always Know,
the meaning of each event,
but embracing your creations,
is frustration you prevent.
Many get confused,
"I did not ask for this",
see the Divine Order,
to lead to greater bliss.

LAW OF
ATTRACTION

As part of manifesting,
here is more detail,
why energies can "move",
while others will "prevail".
Like energies attract the same,
where opposites oppose,
refocus on something new,
the "old" no longer shows.

See two Loving friends,
one suddenly will change,
their energies now repel,
no desires to exchange.
Attraction makes your "luck",
each creates their own,
determined as "good" or "bad",
by the Love that's Known.

INTENT

Creating starts with intent,
for anything you choose,
the energies put out there,
attract and then fuse.
Even if you don't believe,
and Faith is but a little,
intent sets in motion,
this creative "riddle".

Not all intent will manifest,
due to "Higher" cause,
while minimal passion,
creates as if on pause.
Know at any thought,
the creating will start,
a fun game this can be,
if played from the Heart.

MAGIC

To label what's mysterious,
or how it came about,
is magic expressed,
when it is in doubt.
This word is often used,
by some to impress,
or by those who've forgotten,
the Power they suppress.

If everyone remembered,
their "Power-filled days",
there wouldn't be surprise,
by any of these displays.
Whatever you imagine,
can absolutely "be",
focused imagination,
with Faith you will "See".

HEALERS

A "healer" is a channeler,
that's vibrationally high,
that offers cell reminders,
of Perfection to live by.
All healing is mental,
Faith makes it real,
most is subconscious,
that some may not feel.

Sharing high vibrations,
is a guide to "clients",
increasing their awareness,
to see their Self-alliance.
Massaging someone's back,
or rubbing their knee,
is the intent of "healing",
that can work wonderfully.

SACREDNESS

Everything is "sacred",
as All comes from One,
an extension of God,
to never be undone.
To recognize as precious,
this "We" understand,
yet Know All is beautiful,
True in every land.

To live by "sacredness",
is seeing All as such,
that broadens appreciation,
with everything you touch.
Feel your deepest Love,
for your greatest treasure,
turn that to your-Self,
for eternal "sacred" pleasure.

CEREMONY

All forms of ceremony,
that often repeat,
are types of attachment,
where fear is at the seat.
To honor or protect,
are extremes of fear,
Faith in "natural" flow,
makes these disappear.

Ceremony for prevention,
of anything to occur,
blocks the Self "lessons",
you came to endure.
These experiences chosen,
return in different form,
until they are understood,
and flow with your norm.

PROTECTION

In every dimension,
Love will protect,
the degree of its Power,
is Faith you direct.
From Arc Angel "swords",
to Love you project,
this Light "slices through",
trouble you detect.

The need for protection,
is what you make real,
choose to live in Love,
protected you can feel.
With any situation,
you can reflect the fears,
with your Faith and Love,
darkness "disappears".

GUIDANCE

Guidance is directing,
to the Self within,
for the True experience,
you've come to begin.
The "best" way to help,
with someone's questions,
guide them to answering,
with their own suggestions.

Guidance is always flowing,
like a tutor inside of you,
if you choose to listen,
more Wisdom will accrue.
If someone asks a question,
and you choose to share,
you guide as a messenger,
of Light and Loving care.

MESSENGERS

Messengers are required,
for arousing consciousness,
when listening to your-Self,
has become tedious.
When you understand,
any message shared,
you go to another stage,
less mentally impaired.

When the mind is occupied,
with no time for peace,
Self-clarity is minimal,
True listening you cease.
Some "forget" them-Selves,
so remind "We" often do,
messengers are everywhere,
as Loving guides to you.

OUTSIDE SOURCES

Seeking "outside" help,
is Self you ignore,
perceptions from another,
cause your own detour.
"We" are not referring,
to anyone that guides,
but copying another path,
where your-Self hides.

Seminars or books,
including this you read,
may they only guide you,
so you can Self-proceed.
To connect with the "Inside",
is your shortest way,
to experiencing Desircs,
without further delay.

COMPENSATION

There's a financial balance,
each "healer" will find,
of Integrity and Love,
with their "needy" kind.
Some choose not to charge,
others get what they may,
it is your decision,
if it's worth your pay.

To not ask for money,
for a service rendered,
begins a deeper Faith,
where you've Surrendered.
You stop fighting illusions,
of money that appear,
by understanding "Payments",
will always be there.

WEALTH

When most discuss wealth,
money they refer,
yet more begin to realize,
Love they prefer.
May you see that wealth,
can be many things,
like beauty in your life,
that Awareness brings.

Your health is another,
and justifiably so,
your body is a temple,
for the "experience show".
Know you have access,
to Truly anything,
your wealth of Spirit-Mind,
is greater than any king.

HABITS

All people of this world,
live as they know,
some "creatures of habit",
are a re-occurring show.
Often those of habit,
Know not what they do,
like robotic addictions,
of fears coursing through.

These "thoughtless" patterns,
can be reversed,
to reprogram another path,
Desire must be first.
Do it for excitement,
or freedom Self-expressed,
whatever is your reason,
more joy you will attest.

CHANGE

Change is eternal,
which varies in degree,
may everyone embrace it,
showing flexibility.
To some it can be scary,
because of the unKnown,
Faith in the "bigger Picture",
aids the flow and tone.

Those set in their ways,
require dramatic "Signs",
because subtle reminders,
are ignored by their minds.
To listen to your-Self,
don't ignore your "feel",
change will be less shocking,
by listening with zeal.

FLOW

Flowing is to follow,
experience direction,
from the inner-Self,
with no rejection.
If you deny the flow,
fighting each surprise,
joy upon this planet,
you severely compromise.

Going with the flow of life,
is flexibility shown,
where any situation,
has less emotional tone.
To understand your life,
with minimal confusion,
flow with all you can,
for less illusion.

COURAGE

Ohhh precious beings,
the courage you express,
following your passions,
an honor to witness.
You experience unKnown,
with joy or a fight,
yet Know you always have,
partners "in the Light".

"We" can see the beauty,
in every step you take,
following your Desires,
you uniquely make.
Whatever is the outcome,
no failure can be known,
just living on the planet,
is Victory you've shown.

CONFRONTATION

The key to finding answers,
behind any door,
involves using courage,
to return once more.
Confronting is for Truth,
viewed at close range,
experience is transparent,
where details engage.

When "problems" do appear,
confronting can be wise,
to get past the illusions,
that distance supplies.
Whenever you confront,
anything you fear,
you may be surprised,
how it can disappear.

SURRENDER

Surrender to the Truth,
it will free your mind,
destroying weak "walls",
that you live behind.
These illusional barriers,
as your belief base,
imprison you within them,
where your fears you face.

There's no need for shame,
Surrendering to God's "Way",
where you flow with beauty,
and live more True and gay.
It will take much courage,
to drop what you believe,
but Faith will reward you,
with adventure you receive.

STUBBORNNESS

Believing you Know it All,
or resisting Self-guidance,
is blocking "natural" flow,
ignoring "Our" alliance.
The more Aware you are,
the more there is to hear,
it always helps to listen,
with an "open ear".

Some Truth is in the saying,
"I can do it on my own",
yet ego in extremes,
can be what you hone.
In your life experience,
there's always unKnown,
choose to be flexible,
ease you condone.

CONFUSION

When you are confused,
there's inner conflict,
of the flowing Truth,
with fears that restrict.
Your fearful mind blocks,
Desires of your Heart,
by continuing resistance,
discomfort pain will start.

To resist your-Self,
creates a thinking game,
conforming to everyone,
makes True desires lame.
If you live your life,
and follow your Heart,
without worry of others,
confusion will depart.

QUESTIONS

When you ask a question,
it sources of ease,
to go within for Knowledge,
will answer and appease.
There's much Inspiration,
living on "your own",
by answering your questions,
Self-confidence you've shown.

"We" do not shun questions,
it is their clarity,
answers are often Known,
before you make a plea.
"Feel" before you question,
your-Self or anyone,
is it Truly required,
or has boredom begun.

ANGER

Passion with a fear base,
is anger expressed,
Love flow is restricted,
where joy is repressed.
It comes from insecurity,
from belief of Power lost,
a lack of Self-confidence,
or financial cost.

Projecting your anger,
is your reflcctive view,
annoyed by experience,
created by you.
Choose to look within,
for emotions to reverse,
select more understanding,
for anger to disperse.

PAIN

The language Self conveys,
when blockages arise,
is pain to the body,
a warning surprise.
All body aches and pains,
have specific meaning,
less pain will exist,
with your fears' weaning.

Your body is a direct,
extension of the mind,
when pain reaches there,
more severity you find.
May you have the courage,
to look deeply within,
to find your source of pain,
so a reversal can begin.

JEALOUSY

Fear mixed with attachment,
to what another shares,
is jealousy expressed,
with pointed anger flares.
Reliance on the "outside",
for methods of joy,
instead of Loving Self within,
is weakness you employ.

Believing you "don't have",
brings jealousy out,
understand it's All within,
and never will you pout.
When experiencing jealousy,
it's time to detach,
Self-Love instead of grasping,
is your Loving match.

GUILT

Without the perceptions,
of "good and bad",
guilt cannot ever be,
while freedom can be had.
No matter the extreme,
of what you have done,
you're here for experience,
from sadness to fun.

Love is God's essence,
there is no wraith in it,
All have their free-will,
to do as they see fit.
As Creator extensions,
"We" can do no "wrong",
lift this insecurity veil,
confidence will be strong.

GOOD AND BAD

These are mental labels,
as real as believed,
polarities of the Universe,
experientially perceived.
One cannot be Known,
without its counterpart,
to understand this balance,
less judgment you impart.

Equal to "heaven and hell",
they're for order and control,
the fearful use these "tactics",
to belittle or console.
Regain your mental freedom,
no need to redeem,
live the path you choose,
you build your Self-esteem.

BREAKING FREE

Some live amongst you,
unhappy with life,
because of feeling chained,
to situations causing strife.
Being "tied to a desk",
or "the ball and chain",
are examples of captivity,
that need not remain.

Follow Heart's desires,
it Truly sets you free,
cutting all the mental bonds,
allows you just to "be".
By living as you choose,
at your own pace,
is freedom to enjoy,
all that you embrace.

PATIENCE

As you increase awareness,
you will "learn" to wait,
by Knowing All is flowing,
no need to instigate.
This patience you develop,
allows the seeds to sprout,
have Faith in their quality,
more peace will come about.

Nervousness or boredom,
sourced of fear or lull,
both affect your patience,
projecting life as dull.
There is much happening,
that you do not "see",
release "time" attachment,
you become more free.

LAUGHTER

Laughter is so precious,
a beautiful gift to share,
its effects are treasured,
in cultures everywhere.
It is a world "language",
transmuter of all pains,
a sudden joyful downpour,
of beauty that it rains.

Transformer to new levels,
of Awareness Known,
laughing in any way,
keeps you in the zone.
Laughter shatters "walls",
starting communication,
important for experience,
with any known relation.

JOY

An extreme of happiness,
that brings much content,
sourced of peace and Love,
is a "joyful event".
Joy is more profound,
than laughs or happiness,
because it has foundation,
from levels of progress.

Similar to bliss,
a sign of inner peace,
fears are non-existent,
mental thoughts release.
To share is just to "be"
no words you require,
your energies of joy,
are enough to Inspire.

THE
INNER CHILD

Before "right" and "wrong",
is forced into each mind,
there is a guiltless play,
that children often find.
As responsibility comes,
fear transmutes this play,
bills or grades in school,
lead the "child" astray.

Growth is small to large,
not the reverse,
the inner child "should",
expand not disperse.
The beauty of this "child",
is eternal play,
the locator of lost joy,
your guest any day.

PLAY

Jump or dance for joy,
let's go out and play,
your "inner child" exuberance,
desires it this way.
Play the way you choose,
let the "child" come out,
cut loose from the "busy-ness",
yell your "freedom shout".

Frolic in the mountains,
stay within your home,
this playful mental "child",
has anywhere to roam.
Play can be of sounds,
when you speak or sing,
resonance and vibration,
is passion play you bring.

PLEASURE

"What do you like to do",
"We" ask of you today,
whatever is your pleasure,
may you enjoy and play.
Whatever you imagine,
any Heart's Desire,
mentally or physically,
do not let it retire.

Pleasure is of every age,
yet varies in its type,
may you find it everywhere,
and keep desires ripe.
You do not ever need,
to stop what you enjoy,
experience with balance,
and life is your toy.

THE PATH

Some Know their path,
yet fear blocks the flow,
details can be missed,
and the "end" is slow.
Experiences on the path,
are as beautiful as the "finish",
"stop and smell the roses",
apprehensions you diminish.

This path can be a game,
which is lots of fun,
focus your intention,
you've already won.
May you see the beauty,
on every place you land,
you create your "luck",
so joy is at hand.

FREE-WILL

God's "greatest" gift,
is that of free-will,
a reason All is changing,
and not standing still.
There is nothing destined,
free-will makes it so,
follow imagination,
and anything can go.

You're a creative master,
you have endless tools,
you manifest great beauty,
living by your rules.
Create with your Love,
no limits have to be,
follow these True passions,
much new you will "see".

EPILOGUE

This book has offered much,
in reminding many things,
by experiencing any topic,
more Happiness this brings.
This text is a short book,
formatted to reread,
but only as a reference,
for Self-clarity to lead.

The only single "Truth",
you have come here for,
is your Self-experience,
so life you can explore.
Answers are within you,
accessed with Love and fun,
simply do the best you can,
as part of The One.

Eric M. Brodsky
The Universal One Foundation
370 Interlocken Blvd. 4th Fl.
Broomfield, CO 80021

877-OneMind (663-6463) U.S.A.
303-474-1734 Outside the U.S.A.
Website: www.universalone.com

Eric M. Brodsky is the founder of The Universal One Foundation, an international, "non-profit" organization located in Broomfield, Colorado. The organization was founded for the purpose of inspiring people to recognize their own beauty and understand how their love within can lead to great joy and happiness.

The company provides many services, all free of charge, to individuals around the world. This global charity affects all of consciousness by connecting the masses through love and inspiration. It is this Love that we choose to share that integrates Us with . . .

The Universal One.

ORDERING INFORMATION

877-POETRY1 (763-8791) U.S.A.
303-474-1735 Outside the U.S.A.

Please send copies of *Poetry of the Angels II* :
(Please print)

_____to _____
(qty.)   _____

_____to _____
(qty.)   _____

_____ of *Poetry of the Angels* (previous volume)
(qty.) to _____

_____

Enclosed is my check for:

_____ books at US $ 8.00   _____
Shipping/handling $1.50/book: _____

Total   _____

Mail order with check to:

Universal One Publishers
370 Interlocken Blvd. 4th Fl.
Broomfield, CO 80021

http://www.poetryoftheangels.com

READER'S NOTES

READER'S NOTES